ACTION IS THE FOUNDATIONAL KEY TO ALL SUCCESS

Parents, Let's help our little ones learn to be aware and manage their feelings/emotions to eliminate bullying and school violence.

DAVASHI M. SHABAZZ

© 2022 Dictionary.com, LLC,. (n.d.). Emotional Intelligence. Retrived October 1, 2022, from https://www.Dictionary.com.

© You are Mom.com,. (2020). TIPS FOR RAISING YOUR CHILD. Retrived October 1, 2022, from https://www.The Importance of Repetition in Childhood Learning - You are Mom.com.

©MERAKI LANE INC.,. (n.d.). 15 Tips for Parents. In merakilane.com. Retrived October 2, 2022, from https://www.How to Teach Kids About Emotions: 15 Tips for Parents (merakilane.com).com

© Center for Disease Control and Prevention,. (2020). Adolescent and School Health. Retrived October 5, 2022, from https://CDC releases 2019 Youth Risk Behavior Survey Results | Adolescent and School Health | CDC

© Any imagery provided by Canva are models, and such images are being used for illustrative purposes only.© Certain stock imagery via canva.com

Table of Contents:

- Index
  - Parental Information
- Week 1
  - Emotional Intelligence
- Week 2
  - Self Awareness
- Week #3
  - Expression
- Week #4
  - Behavior
    - Social Skills

Index:

- **Word Alert**
  - weekly definition:
    - Emotional Intelligence
    - Self Awareness
    - Expression
    - Behavior
      - Social Skills

- **Benefits of repetition**
  - "Repetition is the foundation for learning skills and goals. It offers children the opportunity to practice an ability or area of knowledge. It teaches children to practice, master, retain, and reinforce knowledge."

- **Parents corner**
  - Goal:
    - This workbook uses pictures to help children connect a feeling with a facial expression. This workbook also uses repetition as a tool to help children learn, develop good habits and master understanding their emotions and feelings.

Let's get started...

THIS BOOK BELONGS TO:

Parents' Corner:

Parents, now is the time to help our children develop their emotional intelligence. This workbook uses pictures to help children connect a feeling with a facial expression. This workbook also uses repetition as a tool to help children learn, develop good habits and master understanding their emotions and feelings. Let's get started and work together...

TIPS TO MOTIVATE YOUR CHILD TO BE AWARE OF THEIR EMOTIONS

COMMUNICATION

- Allow them to talk about their feelings
- Talking through problems helps them see things differently.

EXPRESSION

Find ways for your child to express their emotions
- Journaling: allows them to honestly write about their feelings
- Activity: allows them to be productive and release emotions
- Art: allows them to express their feelings through drawing, painting, etc
- Music: allows them to both feel and release emotions

REFLECTION

Ask Questions about their day:
- Allow them to tell you about situations they faced during the day

Find out :
- If their behavior was appropriate?
- If they could have handled the situation better?

WEEK # 1

Parents, in a child's development, learning about emotions and how to express emotions is very important. Do you remember growing up hearing adults say 'use your words' as a way to encourage you to verbalize (express) how you felt? Do you also remeber feeling confused? Well, the skill of 'using your words' has to be taught and learned. Adults teach and children learn... This week, we will focus on understanding emotions - let's get started.

Parents, how do you feel today?

Emotional Intelligence: The ability to be aware of your own emotions and the emotions of others

LET'S DEVELOP OUR EMOTIONS:
How do you feel today?

- Self Awareness - how do you feel?
- Expression - can you explain why you feel that way?
- Behavior - how are you expressing your feelings to others? (example: when you are sad - are you treating others negatively?)

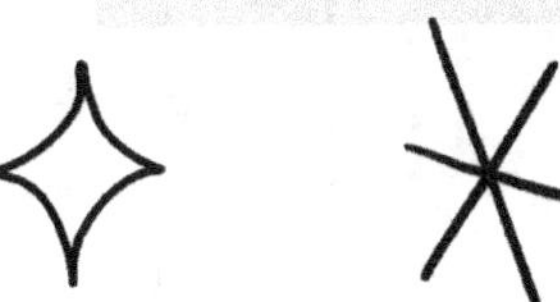

FINAL THOUGHT:

MONDAY – FRIDAY

How are you feeling today?

Your feelings can change throughout the day. Think about how you were feeling in the morning (before school), the afternoon (during school), and right now - what kind of emotions did you experience? Circle the word or words that describe how you were feeling throughout your day. Next, draw the facial expression that shows your feelings throughout your day.

Feelings:

Happy	Worried	Bored	Tired	Sad
Excited	Scared	Irritated	Sick	Frustrated
Creative	Confused	Angry	Nervous	Playful

	Monday	Tuesday	Wednesday	Thursday	Friday
Morning					
Afternoon					
Evening					

Move it Monday

Rise and Shine!

TIME TO GET MOVING:
1. WASH YOUR FACE
2. BRUSH YOUR TEETH
3. EAT A HEALTHY BREAKFAST
4. GET DRESSED

DEALING WITH FEELINGS

Directions: Use your green, yellow and red color crayons for this activity.

GREEN = Calm   Yellow = Sad   RED = Angry

What COLOR are you feeling today?

Green - Calm

Yellow - Sad

Red - Angry

When you start to feel Angry (red color)
Try the below steps to help your emotions get back to calm (green color).

Look at the activities below. Cirlce the picture(s) that can help you get back to feeling calm (green color)

STOP

THINK

BREATHE

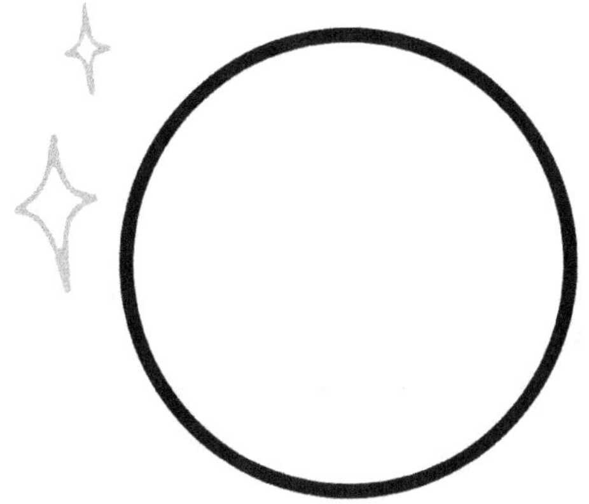

Draw how you feel today

Learning Emotional Intelligence

TODAY I FEEL

SELF AWARENESS

How do you feel______________?

- - - - - - - - - - - - - - - - -

BEHAVIOR

How are you treating others when you feel _____________?

____

- - - - - - - - - - - - - - - - -

EXPRESSION

Can you explain why you feel that way?

____

____

- - - - - - - - - - - - - - - - -

DO YOU UNDERSTAND YOUR FEELINGS?

JOURNAL:

DAY 2

Grateful Tuesday

Being grateful is focusing on what is good in your life, and being thankful for what you have.

Write a note for the person you are thankful for today

- - - - - - - - - -

- - - - - - - - - -

- - - - - - - - - -

DEALING WITH FEELINGS

Directions: Use your green, yellow and red color crayons for this activity.

GREEN = Calm   Yellow = Sad   RED = Angry

What COLOR are you feeling today?

STOP:
BE AWARE OF YOUR FEELINGS

THINK:
HOW DO YOU FEEL
______________?

BREATHE:
WHAT CAN YOU DO
TO FEEL BETTER?

Green - Calm

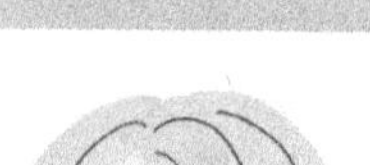

Yellow - Sad

Red - Angry

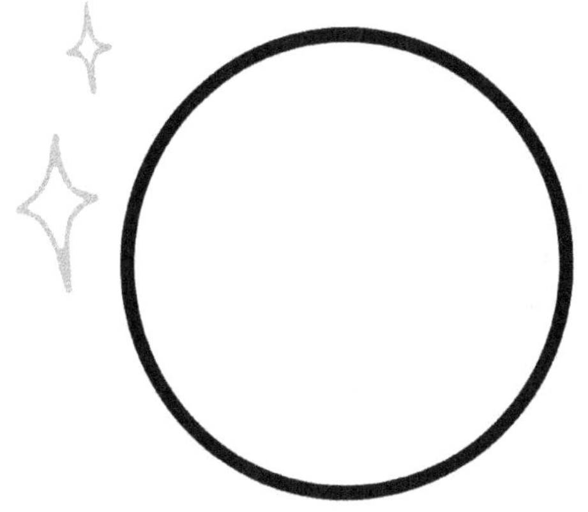

Draw how you feel today

TODAY I FEEL...

SELF AWARENESS

How do you
feel___________________?

BEHAVIOR

How are you treating others
when you feel? _______________

EXPRESSION

Can you explain why you
feel that way?

____

____

DO YOU UNDERSTAND YOUR FEELINGS?

JOURNAL:

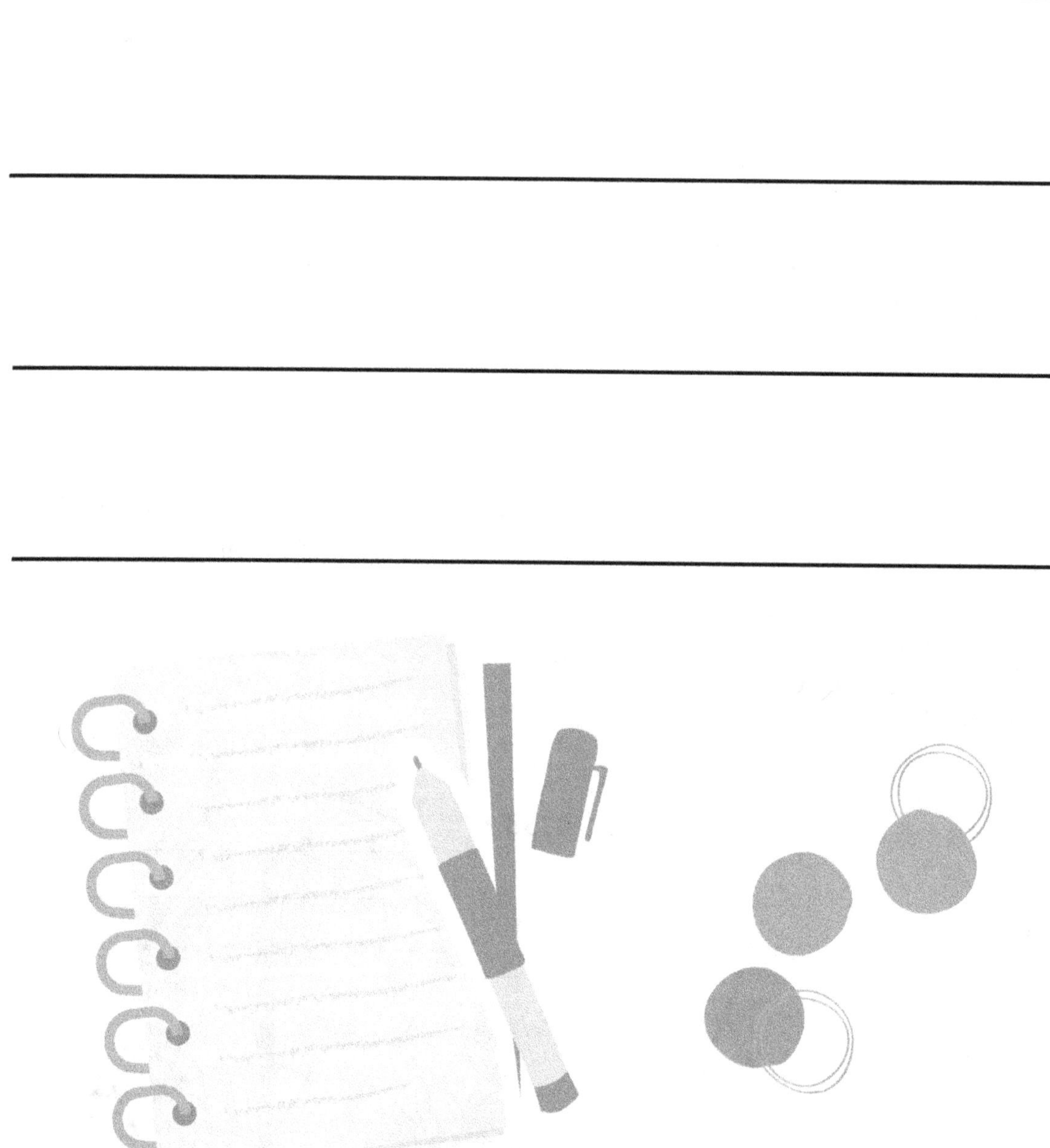

DAY 3

Wacky Wednesday

Let's dress up!
Practice your funny face!
Put on an unusual hat!

DEALING WITH FEELINGS

Directions: Use your green, yellow and red color crayons for this activity.

GREEN = Calm   Yellow = Sad   RED = Angry

What COLOR are you feeling today?

Green - Calm

Yellow - Sad

Red - Angry

When you start to feel Angry (red color)
Try the below steps to help your emotions get back to calm (green color)

Look at the activities below. Cirlce the picture(s) that can help you get back to feeling calm (green color)

STOP

THINK

BREATHE

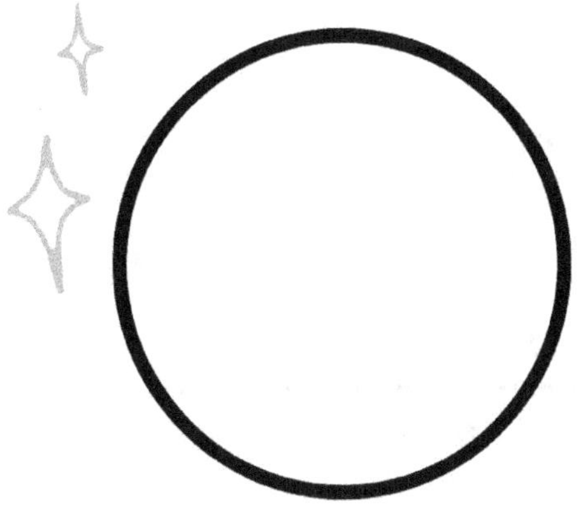

Draw how you feel today

TODAY I FEEL

- SELF AWARENESS
- BEHAVIOR
- EXPRESSION

DO YOU UNDERSTAND YOUR FEELINGS?

SELF AWARENESS

How do you feel________________?

BEHAVIOR

How are you treating others when you feel? ________________

EXPRESSION

Can you explain why you feel that way?

____
____

JOURNAL:

___

___

___

___

___

DAY 4

Thoughtful Thursday

Being thoughtful is about thinking of others, and doing something kind for them. Make someone smile today.

Give them a snack

Offer your help

DEALING WITH FEELINGS

Directions: Use your green, yellow and red color crayons for this activity.

GREEN = Calm   Yellow = Sad   RED = Angry

What COLOR are you feeling today?

When you start to feel Angry (red color)
Try the below steps to help your emotions get back to calm (green color)

STOP:
BE AWARE OF YOUR
FEELINGS

THINK:
HOW DO YOU FEEL

_____________?

BREATHE:
WHAT CAN YOU DO
TO FEEL BETTER?

Green - Calm

Yellow - Sad

Red - Angry

Look at the activities below. Cirlce the picture(s) that can help you get back to feeling calm (green color)

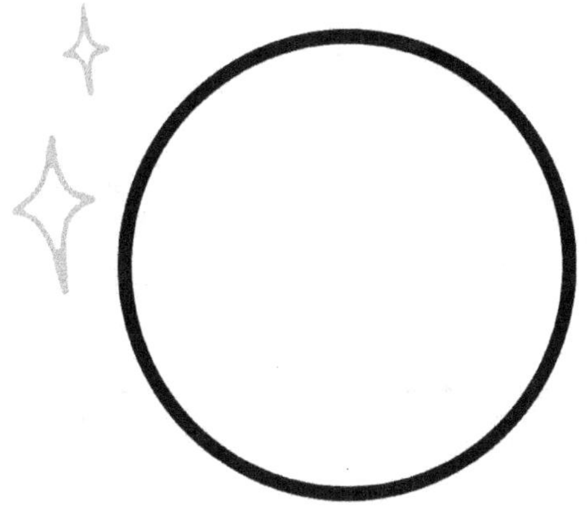

Draw how you feel today

TODAY I FEEL

- -

- -

- -

- SELF AWARENESS
- BEHAVIOR
- EXPRESSION

DO YOU UNDERSTAND YOUR FEELINGS?

SELF AWARENESS

How do you feel_________________?

- - - - - - - - - - - - - - - - - -

BEHAVIOR

How are you treating others when you feel? _______________

- - - - - - - - - - - - - - - - - -

EXPRESSION

Can you explain why you feel that way?

____

____

- - - - - - - - - - - - - - - - - -

JOURNAL:

DAY 5
FRIENDSHIP FRIDAY

How to be a friend

Work together

Keep promises

DEALING WITH FEELINGS

Directions: Use your green, yellow and red color crayons for this activity.

GREEN = Calm   Yellow = Sad   RED = Angry

What COLOR are you feeling today?

Green - Calm

Yellow - Sad

Red - Angry

When you start to feel Angry (red color)

Try the below steps to help your emotions get back to calm (green color)

Look at the activities below. Cirlce the picture(s) that can help you get back to feeling calm (green color)

STOP

THINK

BREATHE

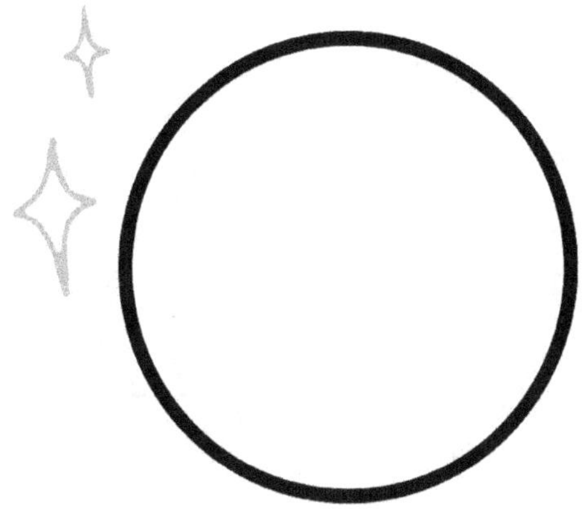

Draw how you feel today

TODAY I FEEL

---- ---- ---- ---- ---- ----

---- ---- ---- ---- ---- ----

---- ---- ---- ---- ---- ----

- **SELF AWARENESS**
- **BEHAVIOR**
- **EXPRESSION**

SELF AWARENESS

How do you feel________________?

- - - - - - - - - - - -

BEHAVIOR

How are you treating others when you feel? ________________

- - - - - - - - - - - -

EXPRESSION

Can you explain why you feel that way?

____

____

- - - - - - - - - - - -

DO YOU UNDERSTAND YOUR FEELINGS?

JOURNAL:

____

____

____

____

____

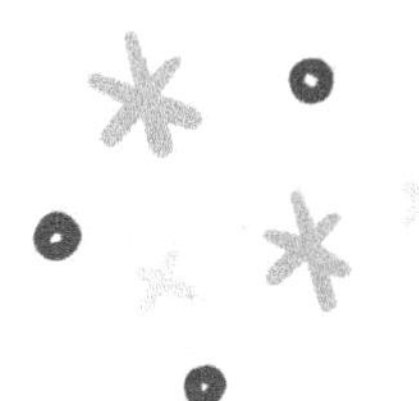

TIPS TO HELP YOUR CHILD MANAGE THEIR EMOTIONS & FEELINGS

01. Teach them to create healthy relationships

02. Help them to recognize their own feelings

03. Help them make good choices

04. Help them not to overreact (self control)

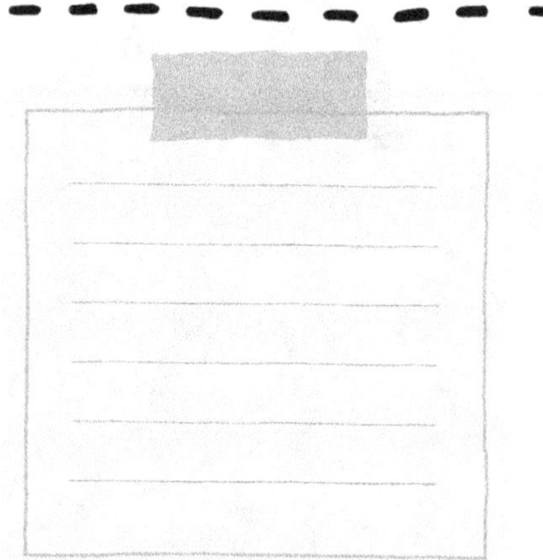

WEEK # 2

Parents, your child's ability to recognize their thoughts, feelings and emotions is very important. We must teach our children to be aware of their feelings, help them name their feelings, and teach them the correct way to express their feelings. This week, we will focus on self awareness – let's get started.

Parents, how do you feel today?

- - - - - - - - - - - - - - - - - - - -

- - - - - - - - - - - - - - - - - - - -

Self Awareness: Recognizing one's own thoughts, feelings and emotions

LET'S DEVELOP OUR EMOTIONS:
How do you feel today?

- - - - - - - - - - - - - - - - - -

- - - - - - - - - - - - - - - - - -

- - - - - - - - - - - - - - - - - -

FINAL THOUGHT: - - - - - - - - - - - - - -

- **Self Awareness - how do you feel?**
- Expression - Can you explain why you feel that way?
- Behavior - how are you expressing your feelings to others? (example: when you are happy, are you treating others nicely?)

MONDAY - FRIDAY

How are you feeling today?

Your feelings can change throughout the day. Think about how you were feeling in the morning (before school), the afternoon (during school), and right now - what kind of emotions did you experience? Circle the word or words that describe how you were feeling throughout your day. Next, draw the facial expression that shows your feelings throughout your day.

Feelings:

Happy Worried Bored Tired Sad

Excited Scared Irritated Sick Frustrated

Creative Confused Angry Nervous Playful

Monday

Tuesday

Wednesday

Thursday

Friday

If you bump
into someone,
say "excuse me"

Do not
interrupt others,
unless it is
an emergency

Do not participate in
name calling

How do you feel today?

Circle the picture or pictures that describe how you were feeling throughout your day.

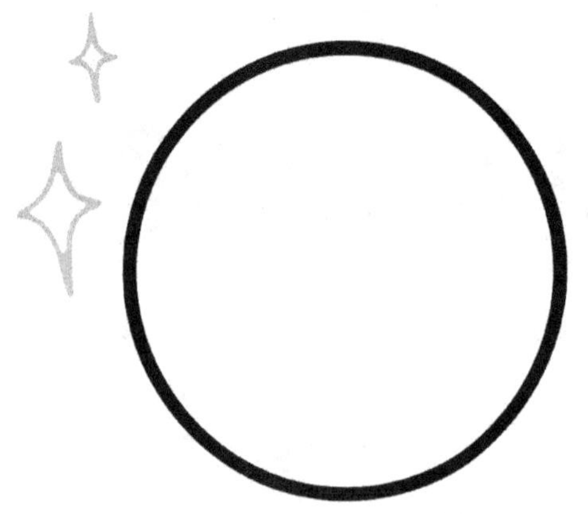

Draw your facial expression

I FEEL

____

BE**CAU**SE

____

- SELF AWARENESS
- BEHAVIOR
- EXPRESSION

THE BEGINNING

What happened in the beginning to make you feel_____________________?

THE MIDDLE

What did you do or say in response?
____
Did you handle the situation good or bad? _____________________________
How are you treating others now that you feel _____________________?

THE END

What was the solution to help you feel better?

____
____

 Draw your face after you have discovered a solution.

JOURNAL:

I FEEL ____

BECAUSE ____

____

____

TO HELP ME FEEL BETTER I AM GOING TO:

____

____

JOURNAL:

Day 2

TOUCH YOUR TOES TUESDAY

Pick a fun activity for a
feel-good day

Exercise

Play with friends

play an instrument

Make art

Read a book

Watch a movie

How do you feel today?

Circle the picture or pictures that describe how you were feeling throughout your day.

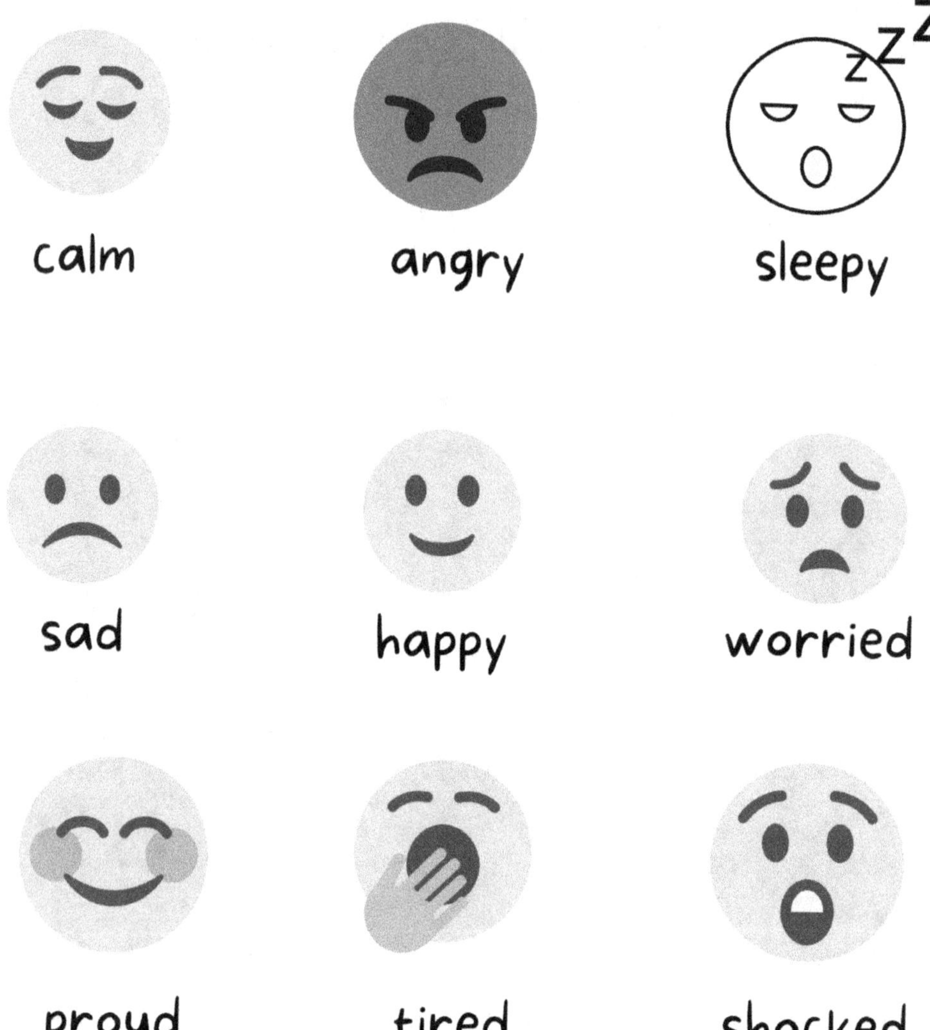

calm	angry	sleepy
sad	happy	worried
proud	tired	shocked

hurt

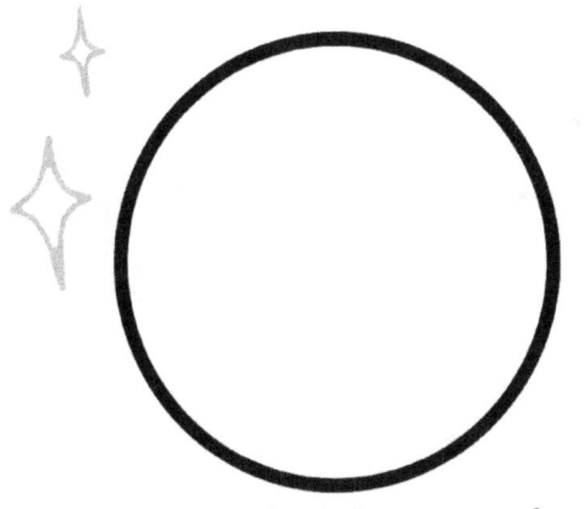

Draw your facial expression

I FEEL

BECAUSE

- - - - - - - - - -

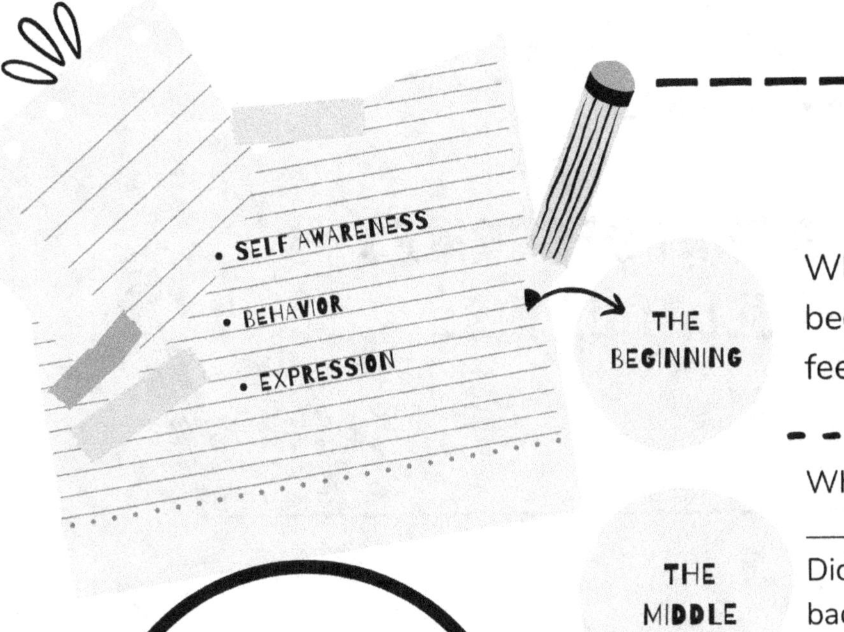

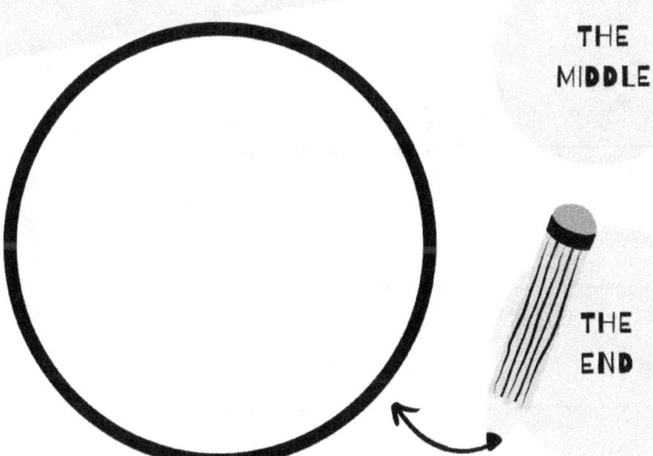

THE BEGINNING

What happened in the beginning to make you feel____________?

THE MIDDLE

What did you do or say in response?
____

Did you handle the situation good or bad? ____________

How are you treating others now that you feel ____________?

THE END

What was the solution to help you feel better?

____

____

Draw your face after you discovered a solution.

JOURNAL:

ONE WORD THAT DESCRIBES
HOW I FEEL TODAY IS:

I FEEL _____________ **BECAUSE:**

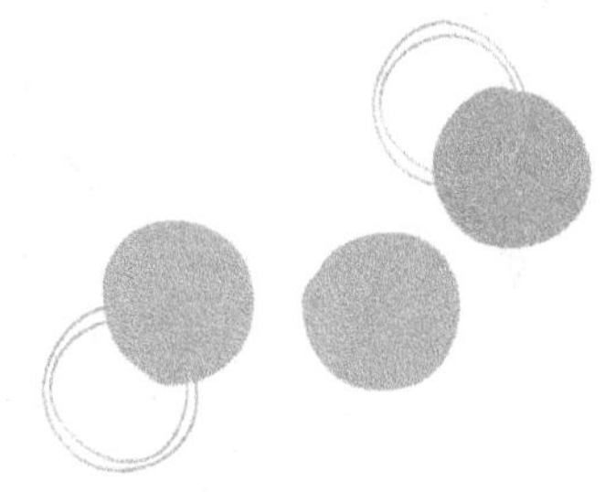

JOURNAL:

DAY 3

Way To Go Wednesday

It's Wednesday,
and you are doing great!

Keep up the good work!!

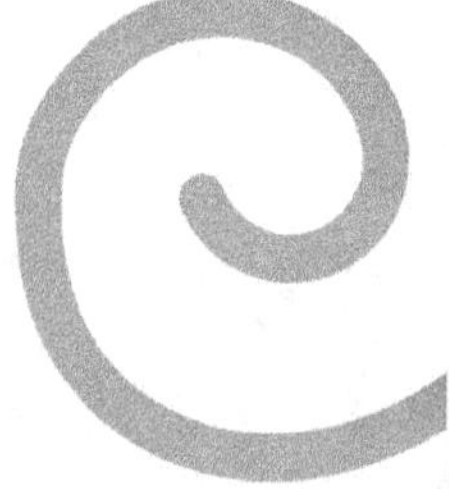

How do you feel today?

Circle the picture or pictures that describe how you were feeling throughout your day.

calm	angry	sleepy
sad	happy	worried
proud	tired	shocked

hurt

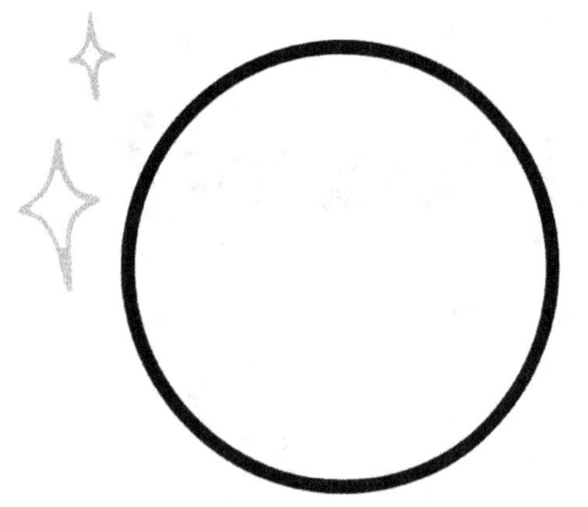

Draw your facial expression

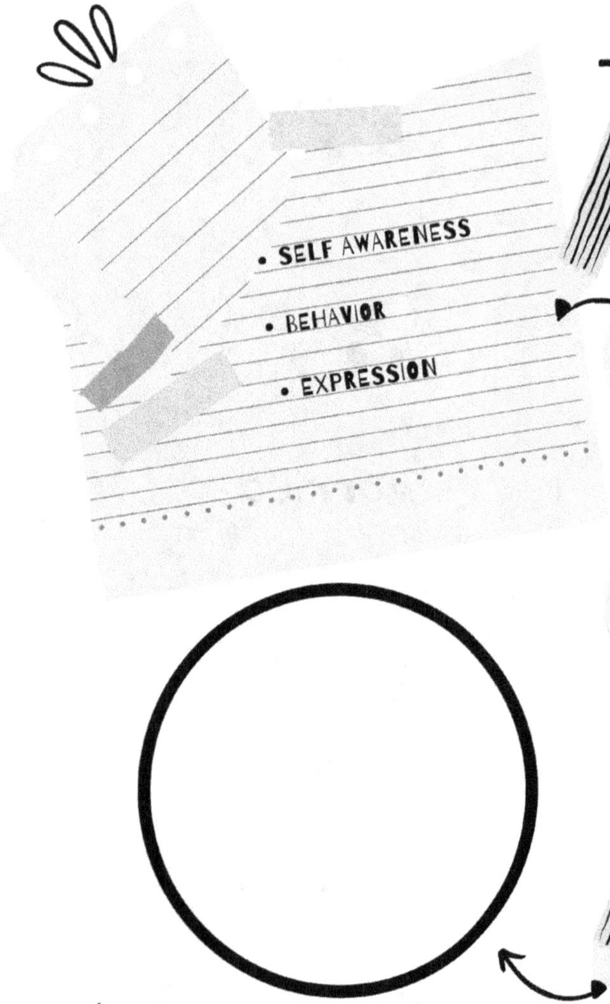

I FEEL

_ _ _ _ _ _ _ _ _ _ _ _ _ _ _ _ _ _ _

BECAUSE

_ _ _ _ _ _ _ _ _ _ _ _ _ _ _ _ _ _ _

- SELF AWARENESS
- BEHAVIOR
- EXPRESSION

THE BEGINNING

What happened in the beginning to make you feel_______________?

THE MIDDLE

What did you do or say in response?
____
Did you handle the situation good or bad? ______________________
How are you treating others now that you feel _______________?

THE END

What was the solution to help you feel better?
____
____

Draw your face after you have discovered a solution.

JOURNAL:

I FEEL ____

BECAUSE ____

____

____

TO HELP ME FEEL BETTER I AM GOING TO:

____

____

JOURNAL:

TRUST THURSDAY

trust yourself

respect others' opinions

be trustworthy

be reliable

be honest

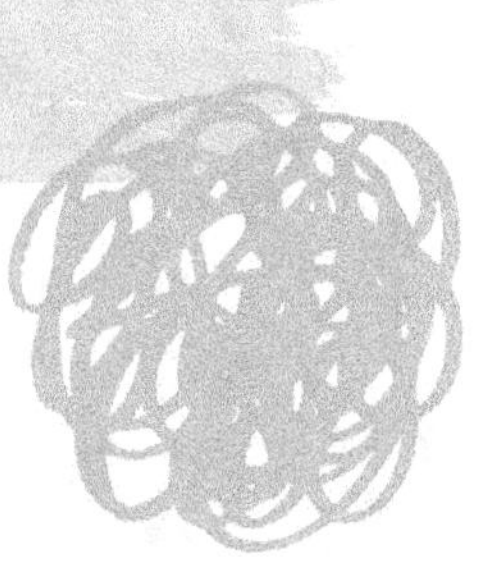

How do you feel today?

Circle the picture or pictures that describe how you were feeling throughout your day.

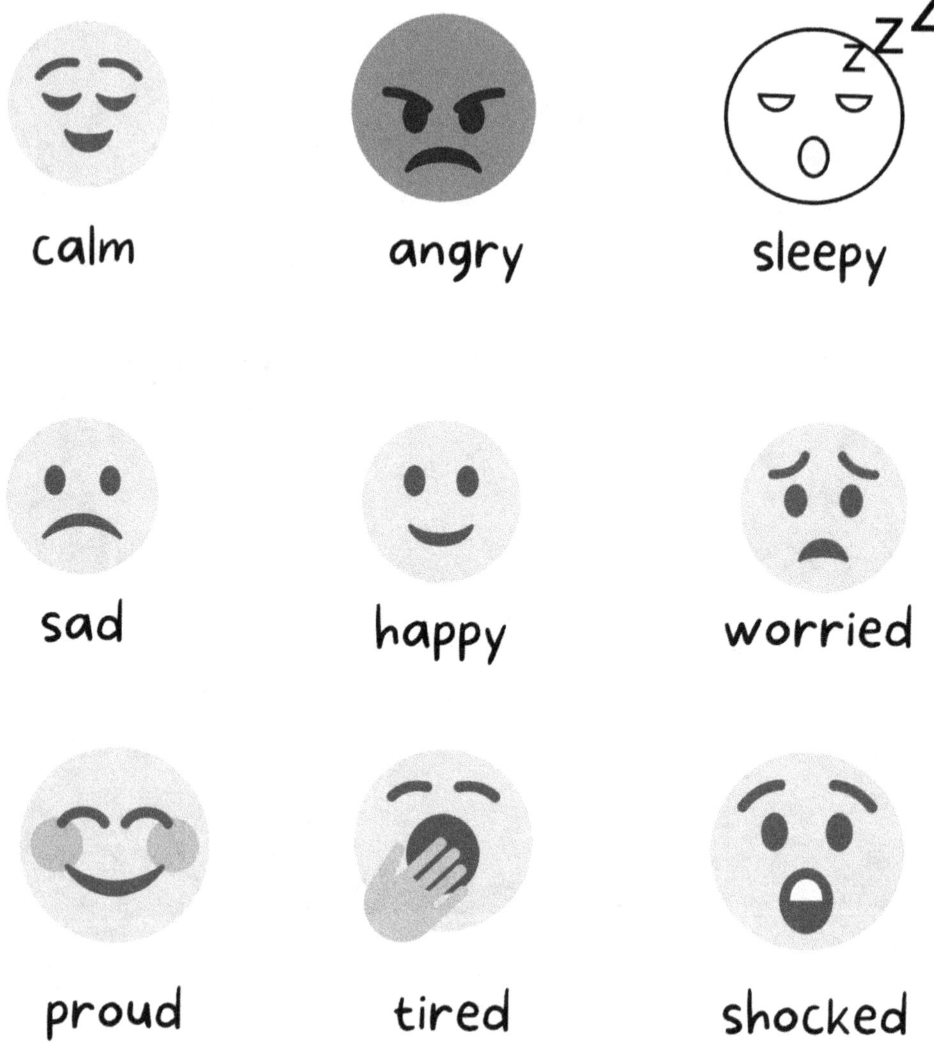

calm   angry   sleepy

sad   happy   worried

proud   tired   shocked

hurt

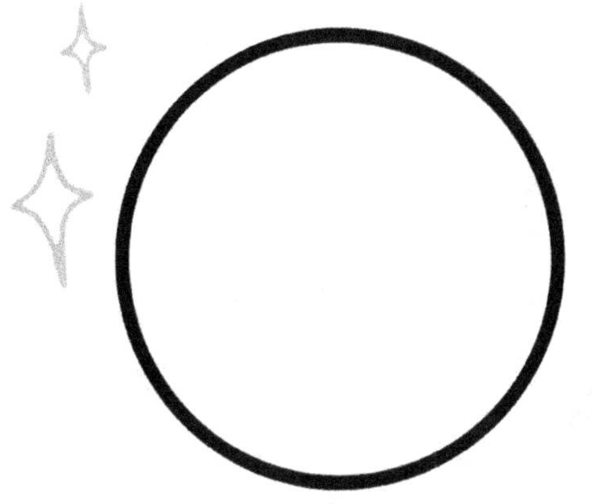

I FEEL

____

BECAUSE

____

Draw your facial expression

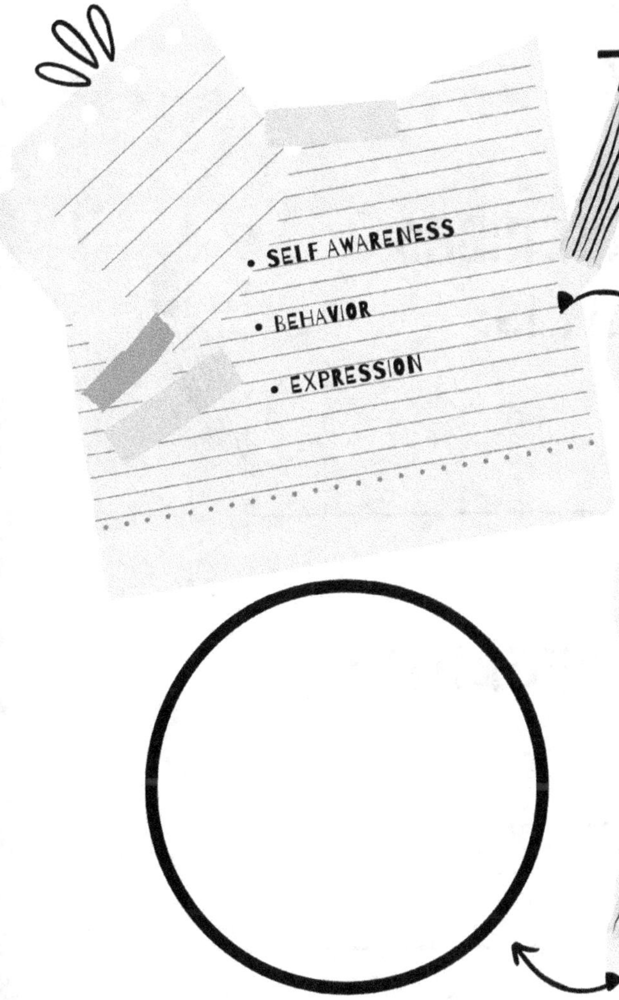

THE BEGINNING

What happened in the beginning to make you feel________________?

What did you do or say in response?
____

THE MIDDLE

Did you handle the situation good or bad? _______________________
How are you treating others now that you feel ________________?

THE END

What was the solution to help you feel better?

____

____

Draw your face after you have discovered a solution.

ONE WORD THAT DESCRIBES
HOW I FEEL TODAY IS:

____

I FEEL ___________ BECAUSE:

____

____

____

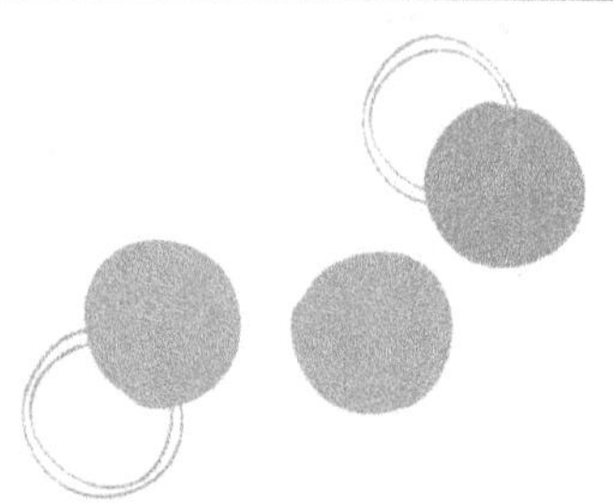

JOURNAL:

____

____

____

____

____

FRIENDSHIP FRIDAY

How to be a friend

How do you feel today?

Circle the picture or pictures that describe how you were feeling throughout your day.

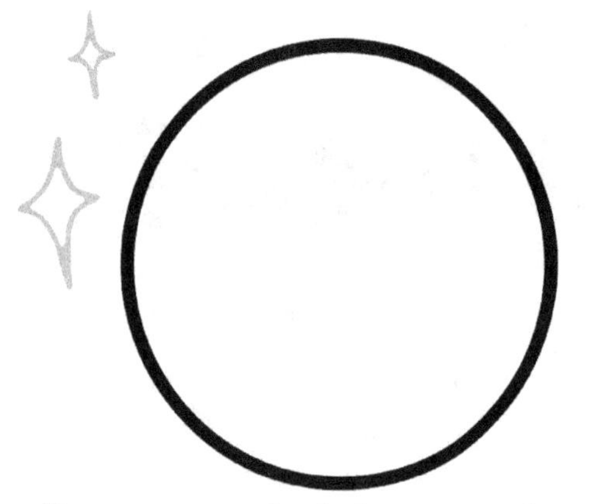

Draw your facial expression

I FEEL

BE**CAU**SE

THE BEGINNING

What happened in the beginning to make you feel_________________?

- - - - - - - - - - - - - - - - - -

THE MIDDLE

What did you do or say in response?
____
Did you handle the situation good or bad? ___________________________
How are you treating others now that you feel _________________?

- - - - - - - - - - - - - - - - - -

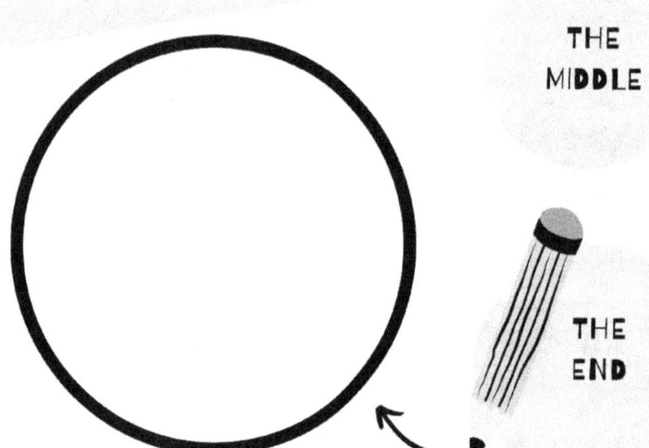

THE END

What was the solution to help you feel better?

____
____

- - - - - - - - - - - - - - - - - -

Draw your face after you have discovered a solution.

I FEEL ________________________________

BECAUSE ________________________________

____

____

TO HELP ME FEEL BETTER I AM GOING TO:

____

____

JOURNAL:

JOURNAL

TIPS TO MOTIVATE YOUR CHILD TO UNDERSTAND AND COMMUNICATE THEIR EMOTIONS

Frustrated

Joy

Anger

Sadness

Fear

DO YOU KNOW YOUR FEELINGS?

- Help them notice & name their feelings
- Track how long they feel that emotion
- Help them remember what they did to feel better
- Learn new words for feelings to help them express themselves
- Encourage them to Journal about their feelings

WEEK # 3

At an early age children began to understand basic emotions. They understand words like happy, mad, sad, and scared. Teaching your child to understand their emotions at an early age will benefit them throughout their young life into adulthood. This week, we will focus on self expression – let's get started.

Parents, how do you feel today?

 **Expression:** The process of making known one's thoughts, feelings, and emotions

LET'S DEVELOP OUR EMOTIONS:
How do you feel today?

- Self Awareness - how do you feel?
- **Expression - can you explain why you feel that way?**
- Behavior - how are you expressing your feelings to others? (example: when you are angry, are you rude/mean to others?)

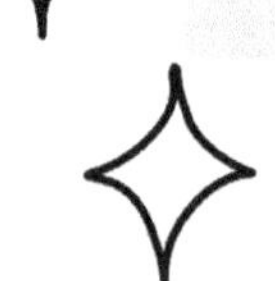 

FINAL THOUGHT: - - - - - - - - - - -

MONDAY – FRIDAY

How are you feeling today?

Your feelings can change throughout the day. Think about how you were feeling in the morning (before school), the afternoon (during school), and right now - what kind of emotions did you experience? For each day of the week, circle and write the word or words that describe how you were feeling for the majority of each day.

Feelings:

Happy	Worried	Bored	Tired	Sad
Creative	Confused	Angry	Nervous	Playful
Excited	Scared	Irritated	Sick	Frustrated

Monday
Today is Monday, and I feel:

Tuesday
Today is Tuesday, and I feel:

Wednesday
Today is Wednesday, and I feel:

Thursday
Today is Thursday, and I feel:

Friday
Today is Friday, and I feel:

 # All About You:

My name is:_______________________________

My birthday is:_______________________________

My address is:_______________________________

My telephone number is:_______________________________

My favorite things:

color: _______________

book:_______________

food:_______________

teacher:_______________

hobby:_______________

store:_______________

TV show:_______________

activity:_______________

When I
grow up I
want to be:

____
____
____

HELLO MONDAY

HAVE A GREAT MONDAY! START THE DAY WITH ENCOURAGEMENT. MOTIVATE AND ENCOURAGE YOURSELF BY SAYING THE BELOW PHRASES:

I AM **LOVED**

I AM **KIND**

I AM **CAPABLE**

I AM **BRAVE**

I AM **ENOUGH**

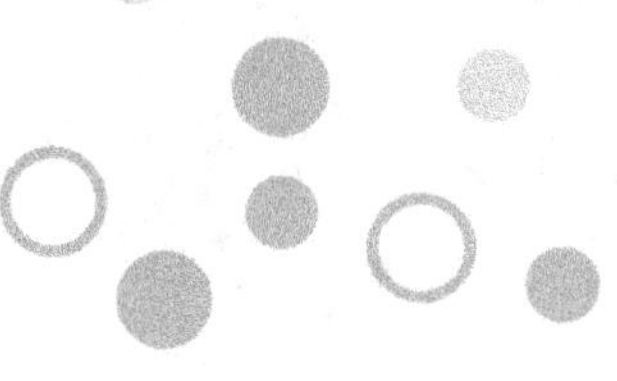

Words for My Feelings

Did you know that there are many words for your feelings? Check them out.

Feeling happy can also mean:

Cheerful
Joyful
Glad
Wonderful

Feeling sad can also mean:

Gloomy
Blue
Down
Unhappy

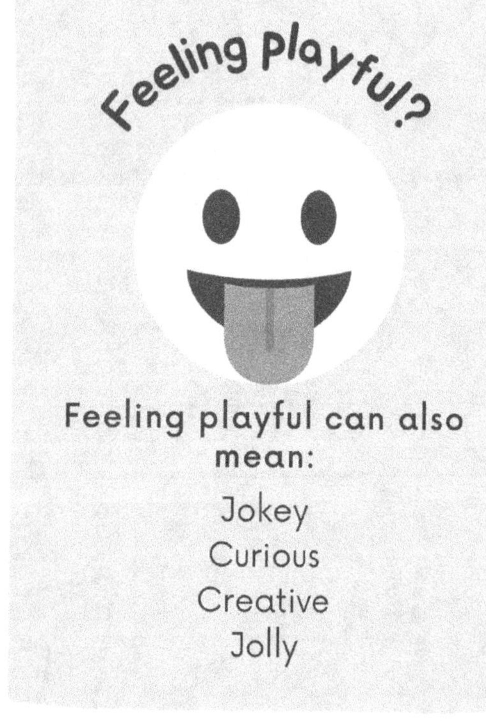

Feeling playful can also mean:

Jokey
Curious
Creative
Jolly

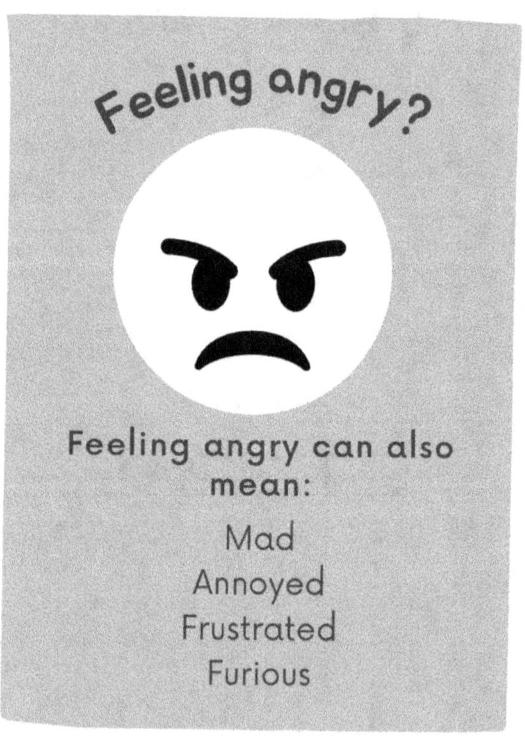

Feeling angry can also mean:

Mad
Annoyed
Frustrated
Furious

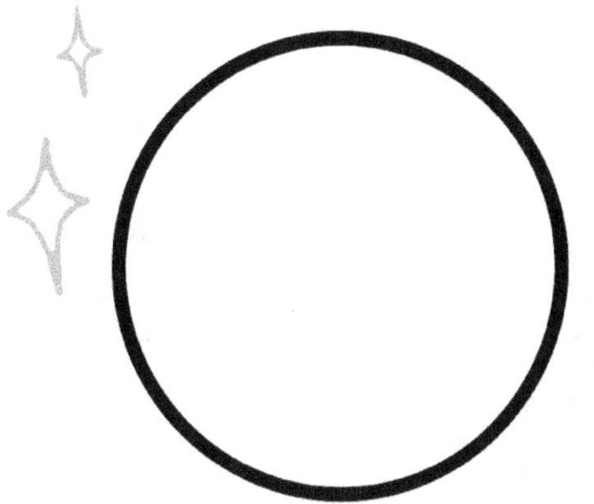

Draw how you made others feel today

BECAUSE I FEEL

I TREATED OTHERS

- SELF AWARENESS
- BEHAVIOR
- EXPRESSION

THE BEGINNING

What happened in the beginning to make you feel_________________?

- - - - - - - - - - -

What did you do or say in response? _____________

____

THE MIDDLE

How are you treating others now that you feel _____________?

- - - - - - - - - - -

THE END

What was the solution to help you feel better?

____

____

- - - - - - - - - - -

HOW ARE YOU TREATING OTHERS?

I PLAYED WITH MY FRIENDS TODAY

I FEEL _______________________________________

BECAUSE WE _______________________________

____

____

THIS IS WHAT I AM GOING TO DO TO MAKE MY FRIENDS SMILE:

____

____

JOURNAL:

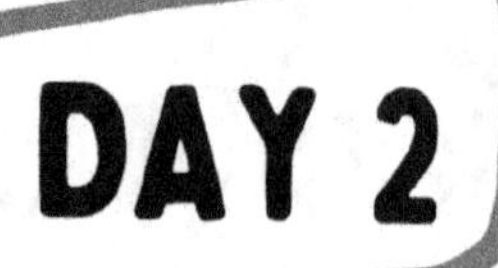

Telling Them Tuesday

Being grateful is focusing on
what is good in your life, and
being thankful
for what you have.

Say something nice to the person
you are thankful for today

<table>
<tr><td>

**You are a
great listener**

</td><td>

**I want to grow
up to be just like
you**

</td></tr>
<tr><td>

**I am happy you
are in my life**

</td><td>

**You are always
helpful**

</td></tr>
</table>

Words for My Feelings

Did you know that there are many words for your feelings? Check them out.

Feeling happy?

Feeling happy can also mean:

Cheerful
Joyful
Glad
Wonderful

Feeling sad?

Feeling sad can also mean:

Gloomy
Blue
Down
Unhappy

Feeling playful?

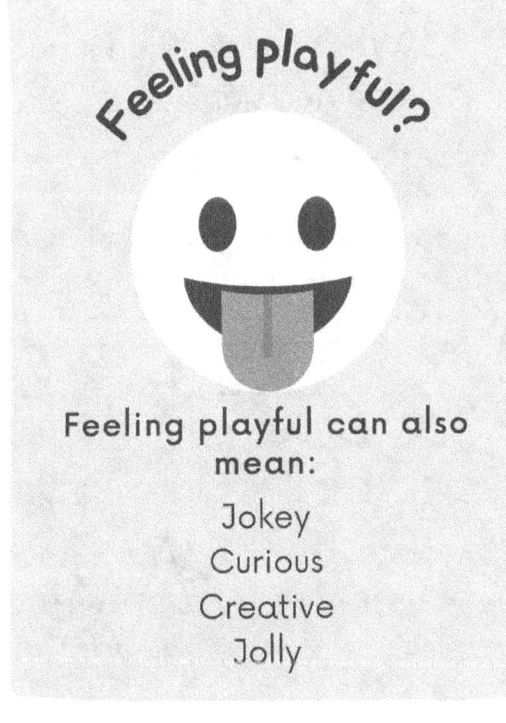

Feeling playful can also mean:

Jokey
Curious
Creative
Jolly

Feeling angry?

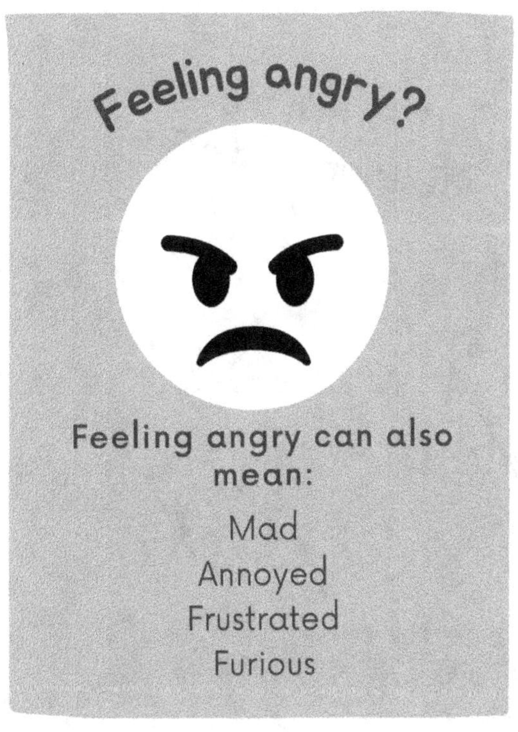

Feeling angry can also mean:

Mad
Annoyed
Frustrated
Furious

Good Decision Journal

I DECIDED TO

____

I FEEL ______________ ABOUT MY DECISION

THE BEGINNING

What happened in the beginning to make you feel________________?

THE MIDDLE

What did you do or say in response? ________________

Was your decision a good or bad decision? ________________

THE END

What was the solution to help you feel better?

____

____

Did you make good decisions today?

JOURNAL:

ONE WORD THAT DESCRIBES HOW I FEEL TODAY IS:

____

I AM FEELING: _______________________________

I AM THINKING ABOUT: _______________

____

RIGHT NOW, I REALLY NEED: _______________________

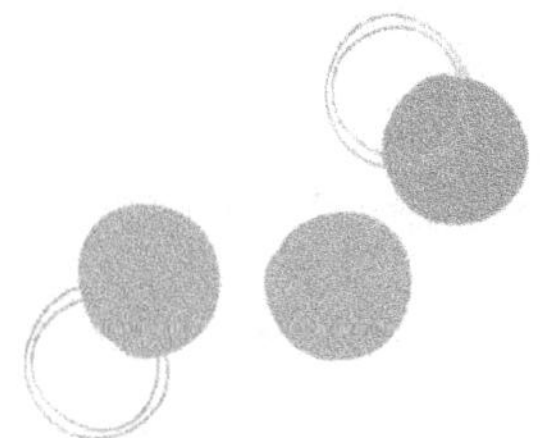

JOURNAL:

WE ARE A TEAM
WEDNESDAY

friends

we respect
each other

we learn
from our
mistakes

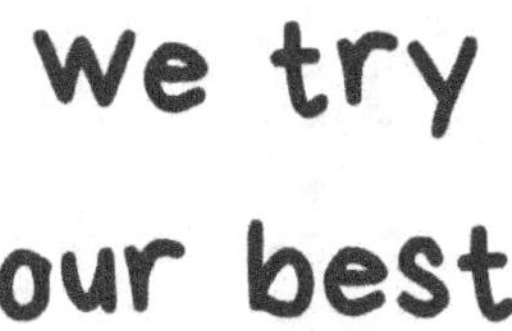

we try
our best

Words for My Feelings

Did you know that there are many words for your feelings? Check them out.

Feeling happy?

Feeling happy can also mean:

Cheerful
Joyful
Glad
Wonderful

Feeling sad?

Feeling sad can also mean:

Gloomy
Blue
Down
Unhappy

Feeling playful?

Feeling playful can also mean:

Jokey
Curious
Creative
Jolly

Feeling angry?

Feeling angry can also mean:

Mad
Annoyed
Frustrated
Furious

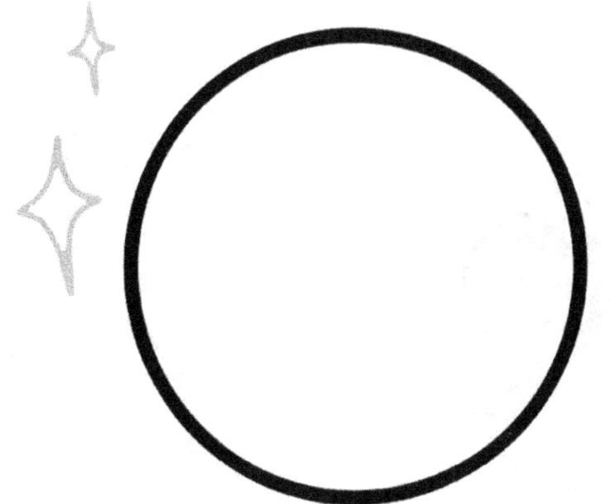

Draw how you made others feel today

Self Expression Journal

BECAUSE I FEEL

____

I TREATED OTHERS

____

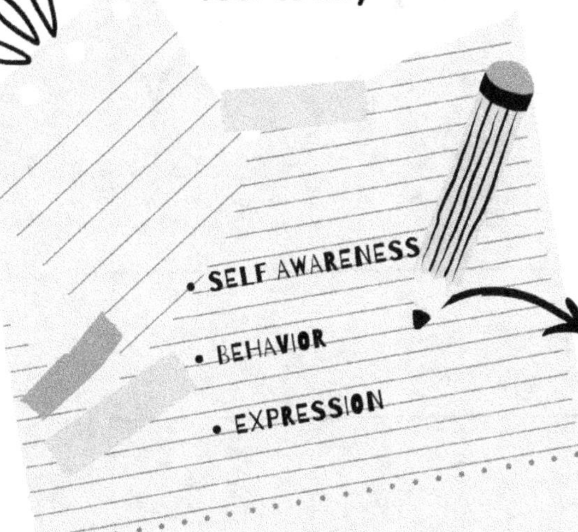

THE BEGINNING

What happened in the beginning to make you feel____________________?

THE MIDDLE

What did you do or say in response?____________________

____

How are you treating others now that you feel ___________?

THE END

What was the solution to help you feel better?

____

____

HOW ARE YOU TREATING OTHERS?

JOURNAL:

I PLAYED WITH MY FRIENDS TODAY

I FEEL _______________________________________

BECAUSE WE _______________________________

____

____

THIS IS WHAT I AM GOING TO DO TO MAKE MY FRIENDS SMILE:

____

____

JOURNAL:

____

____

____

____

____

Think About It Thursday

what can I do to make my friends smile?

What can I do to show my family that I love them?

What can I do to get good grades in school?

What chores can I do to help my parents?

Words for My Feelings

Did you know that there are many words for your feelings? Check them out.

Feeling happy can also mean:

Cheerful
Joyful
Glad
Wonderful

Feeling sad can also mean:

Gloomy
Blue
Down
Unhappy

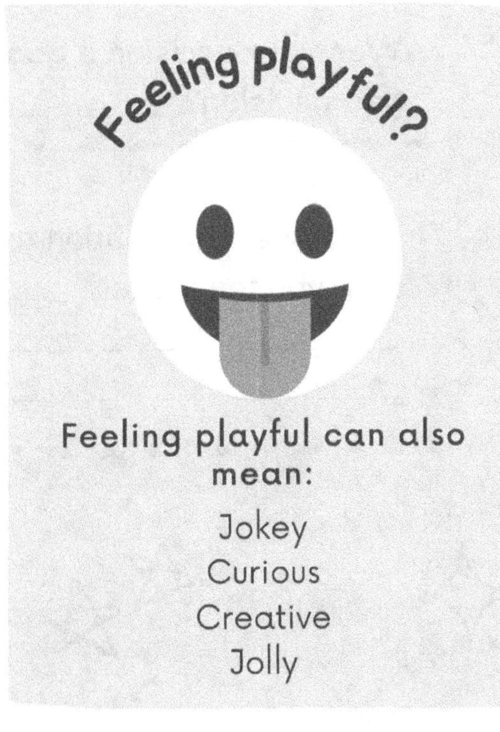

Feeling playful can also mean:

Jokey
Curious
Creative
Jolly

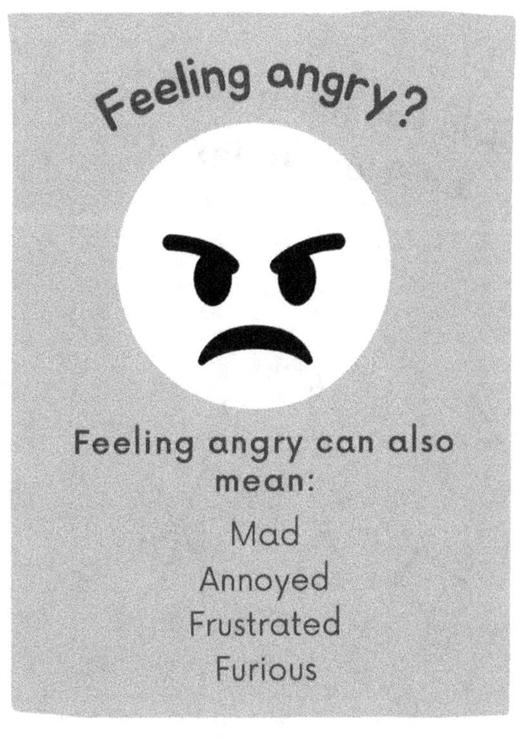

Feeling angry can also mean:

Mad
Annoyed
Frustrated
Furious

I DECIDED TO

____

I FEEL ________________
ABOUT MY DECISION

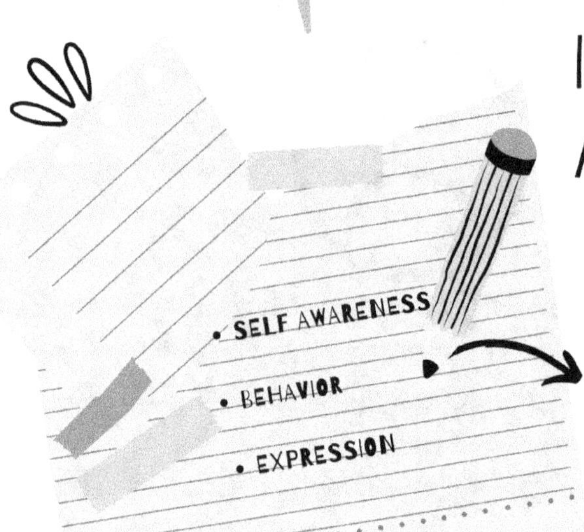

THE BEGINNING

What happened in the beginning to make you feel________________?

- - - - - - - - - - - - -

THE MIDDLE

What did you do or say in response? ________________

Was your decision a good or bad decision? ________________

- - - - - - - - - - - - -

THE END

What was the solution to help you feel better?

____
____

- - - - - - - - - - - - -

Did you make good decisions today?

I FEEL _______________________

BECAUSE _______________________

____

____

TO HELP ME FEEL BETTER I AM GOING TO:

____

____

JOURNAL:

DAY 5
FRIENDSHIP FRIDAY

How to be a friend

Tell the truth

Share what you
have

Words for My Feelings

Did you know that there are many words for your feelings? Check them out.

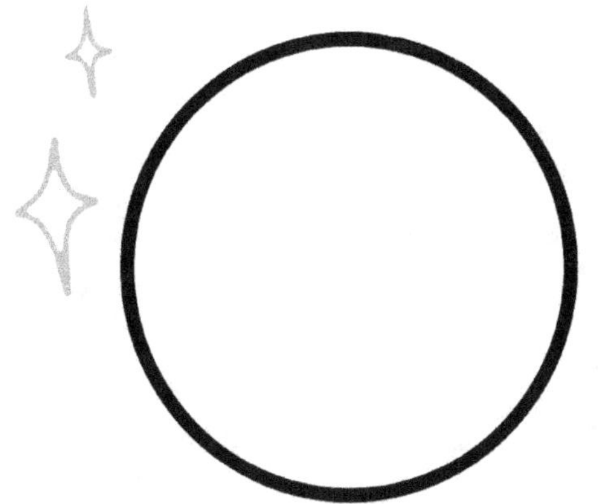

Draw how you made others feel today

BECAUSE I FEEL

I TREATED OTHERS

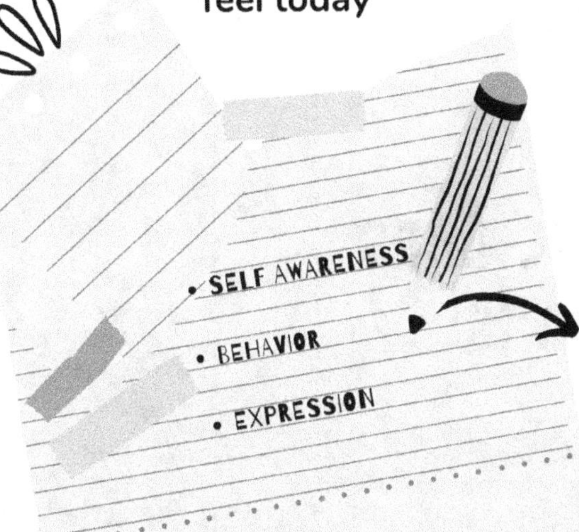

THE BEGINNING

What happened in the beginning to make you feel_________________?

- - - - - - - - - - - - -

THE MIDDLE

What did you do or say in response? ______________
____

How are you treating others now that you feel _______________?

- - - - - - - - - - - - -

THE END

What was the solution to help you feel better?
____
____

- - - - - - - - - - - - -

HOW ARE YOU TREATING OTHERS?

ONE WORD THAT DESCRIBES HOW I FEEL TODAY IS:

____

I FEEL _____________ BECAUSE:

____

____

____

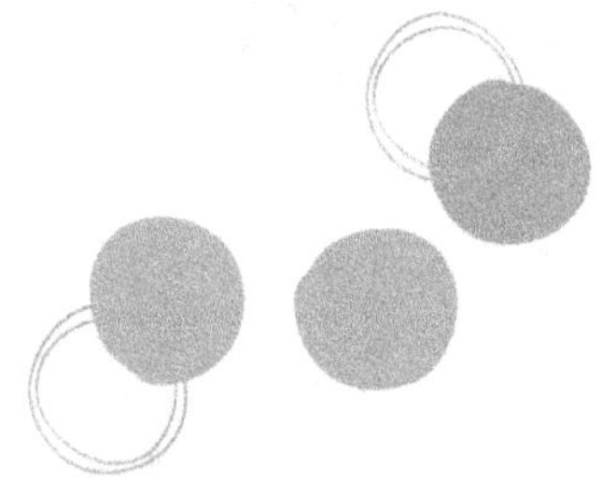

JOURNAL:

WEEK # 4

Great job! Please continue to work with your child regarding understanding their emotions. Use this tool as often as needed to reinforce the good behavior developed while utilizing this workbook. We will continue this week working on communicating with words instead of meltdowns and temper tantrums. Now that they have learned to be aware of their feelings, expressing their feelings, and making good decisions, they will put that work into practice by recognizing their behavior and how they treat others. This week, we will focus on behavior and social skills – let's get started.

Parents, how do you feel today?

Behavior: How are you expressing your feelings to others?

Social Skills: The ability to create and maintain relationships (healthy relationships)

LET'S DEVELOP OUR EMOTIONS:
How do you feel today?

- Self Awareness - how do you feel?
- Expression -Can you explain why you feel that way?
- **Behavior - how are you expressing your feelings to others?** (example: when you are playful - do you ignore instructions from adults and continue to play?)

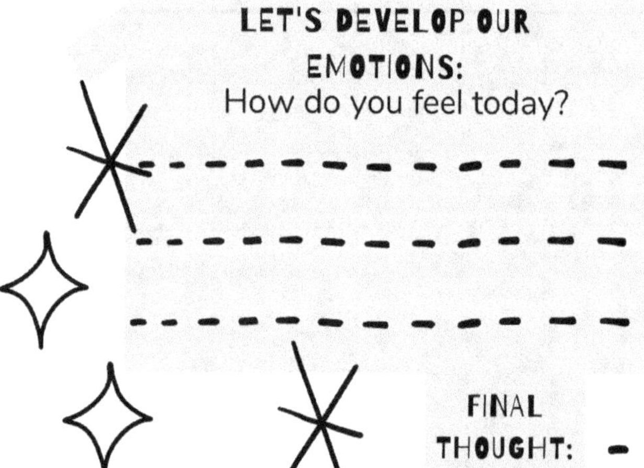

FINAL THOUGHT:

MONDAY – FRIDAY

How are you feeling today?

Your feelings can change throughout the day. Think about how you were feeling in the morning (before school), the afternoon (during school), and right now - what kind of emotions did you experience? Circle the word or words that describe how you were feeling throughout your day. Next, draw the facial expression that shows your feelings throughout your day.

Feelings:

Happy	Worried	Bored	Tired	Sad
Excited	Scared	Irritated	Sick	Frustrated
Creative	Confused	Angry	Nervous	Playful

	Monday	Tuesday	Wednesday	Thursday	Friday
Morning					
Afternoon					
Evening					

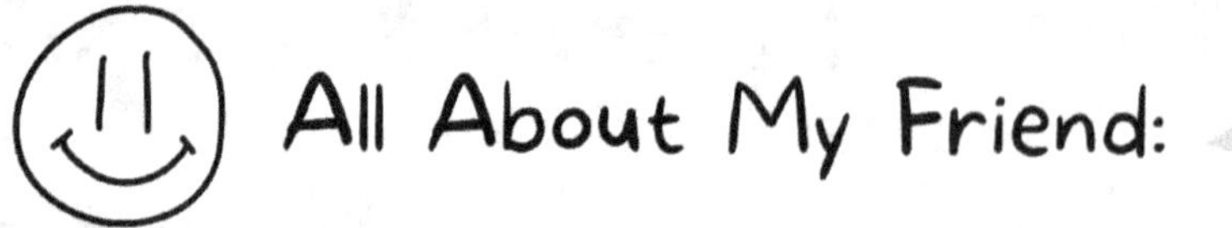 All About My Friend:

What is your Friend's name?_______________________________

What is your Friend's favorite animal?_________________________

Does your Friend have sisters or brothers?__________________

Your friend's favorite things:

color: _______________

book:_________________

food:_________________

teacher:______________

hobby:________________

store:________________

TV show:_____________

activity:______________

What does your friend want to be when he or she grows up?

____

____

Mindful Monday

Smile and be
polite to others

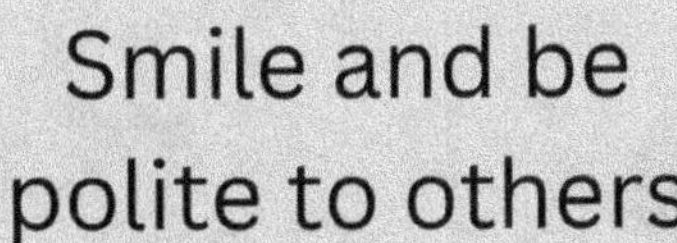

Say, "please
and thank you"

Be respectful

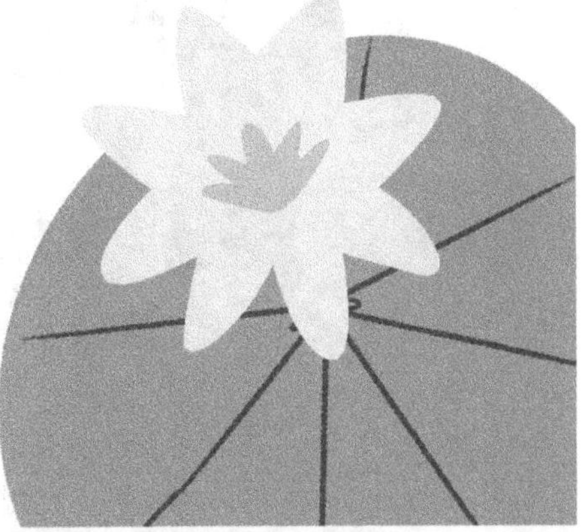

How are you feeling today?

Find the picture or pictures that best describe how you were feeling throughout your day.

PROUD

BORED

CURIOUS

PLAYFUL

TIRED

HUNGRY

ANGRY

WORRIED

SCARED

HAPPY

CONFUSED

NERVOUS

DISGUSTED

ANNOYED

SAD

AMUSED

Draw how your friend(s)
made you feel today

TODAY I TOLD MY FRIENDS THEY MADE ME FEEL

- SELF AWARENESS
- BEHAVIOR
- EXPRESSION

HOW ARE YOU PLAYING WITH OTHERS?

THE BEGINNING

What did your friend(s) do in the beginning to make you feel _________________?

THE MIDDLE

What did you do or say in response? _______________
____

How are you treating others now that you feel ____________?

THE END

What was the solution to help you feel better?
____
____

JOURNAL:

My day was: ___________________________________

My favorite part was: ___________________________________

My worst part was: ___________________________________

My thoughts and concerns about today:

____

____

____

____

Things I can do to feel better:

____

____

____

____

JOURNAL:

DAY 2

Tip Tuesday

WHAT'S YOUR FAVORITE HOLIDAY?

IF YOU COULD BE ANY CARTOON CHARACTER, WHO WOULD IT BE?

DO YOU HAVE BROTHERS OR SISTERS?

CONVERSATION STARTERS

ASK QUESTIONS TO GET TO KNOW YOUR FRIENDS

WHAT SNACKS DO YOU LIKE?

WHAT'S YOUR FAVORITE GAME?

How are you feeling today?

Find the picture or pictures that best describe how you were feeling throughout your day.

PROUD

BORED

CURIOUS

PLAYFUL

TIRED

HUNGRY

ANGRY

WORRIED

SCARED

HAPPY

CONFUSED

NERVOUS

DISGUSTED

ANNOYED

SAD

AMUSED

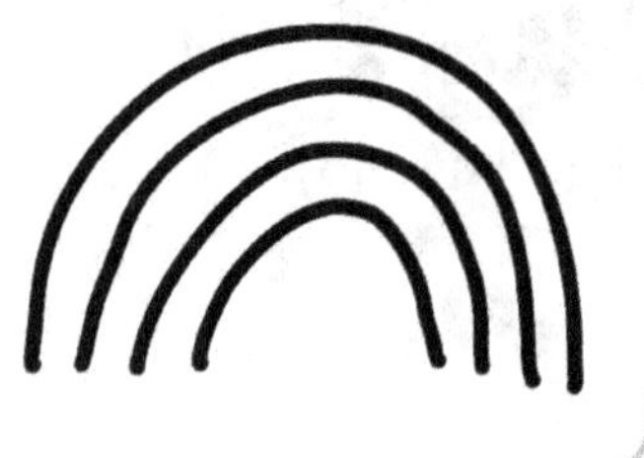

I DECIDED TO

____

I FEEL ______________
ABOUT MY DECISION

THE BEGINNING

What happened in the beginning to make you feel_________________?

THE MIDDLE

What did you do or say in response? _______________

Was your decision a good or bad decision? _____________

THE END

What was the solution to help you feel better?

____

____

Did you make good decisions today?

I FEEL ___________________________________

BECAUSE _________________________________

____

____

TO HELP ME FEEL BETTER I AM GOING TO:

____

____

JOURNAL:

WELL-DONE WEDNESDAY

Learn more
and create

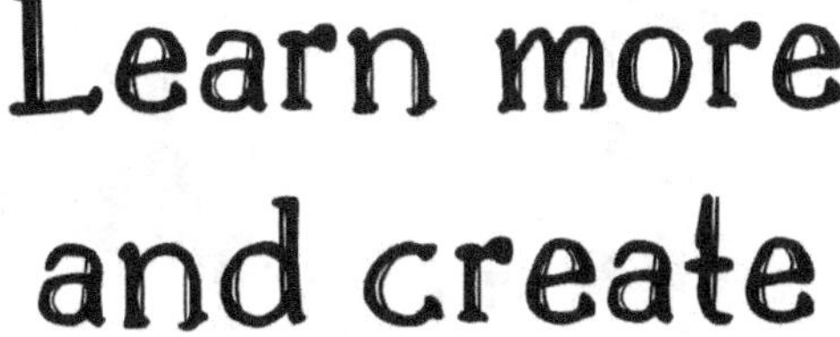

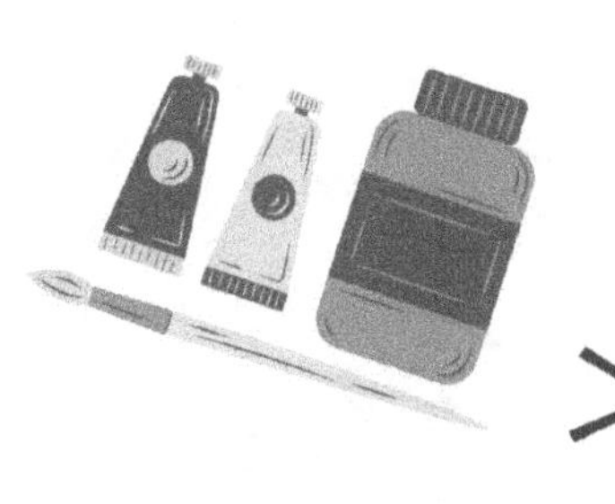

How are you feeling today?

Find the picture or pictures that best describe how you were feeling throughout your day.

PROUD

BORED

CURIOUS

PLAYFUL

TIRED

HUNGRY

ANGRY

WORRIED

SCARED

HAPPY

CONFUSED

NERVOUS

DISGUSTED

ANNOYED

SAD

AMUSED

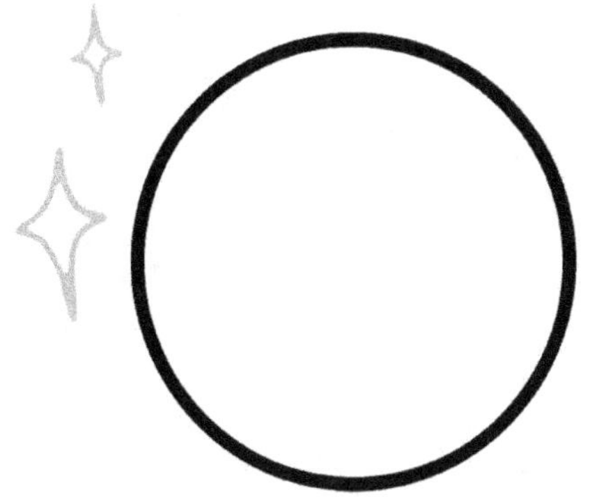

**Draw how your friend(s)
made you feel today**

TODAY I TOLD MY FRIENDS THEY MADE ME FEEL

- - - - - - - - - - - - - - - - - - -

- - - - - - - - - - - - - - - - - - -

- SELF AWARENESS
- BEHAVIOR
- EXPRESSION

THE BEGINNING

What did your friend(s) do in the beginning to make you feel _________________?

- - - - - - - - - - - - - - - - - - -

THE MIDDLE

What did you do or say in response? _______________
____

How are you treating others now that you feel ___________?

- - - - - - - - - - - - - - - - - - -

THE END

What was the solution to help you feel better?
____
____

- - - - - - - - - - - - - - - - - - -

HOW ARE YOU PLAYING WITH OTHERS?

ONE WORD THAT DESCRIBES
HOW I TREATED OTHERS
TODAY IS:

____

I AM FEELING _______________ ABOUT HOW I
TREATED OTHERS TODAY.

I AM THINKING ABOUT: _______________

____

RIGHT NOW, I
REALLY NEED: _______________________

JOURNAL:

Day 4
Thoughtful Thursday

Being thoughtful is about thinking of others and doing something kind for them. Make someone smile today.

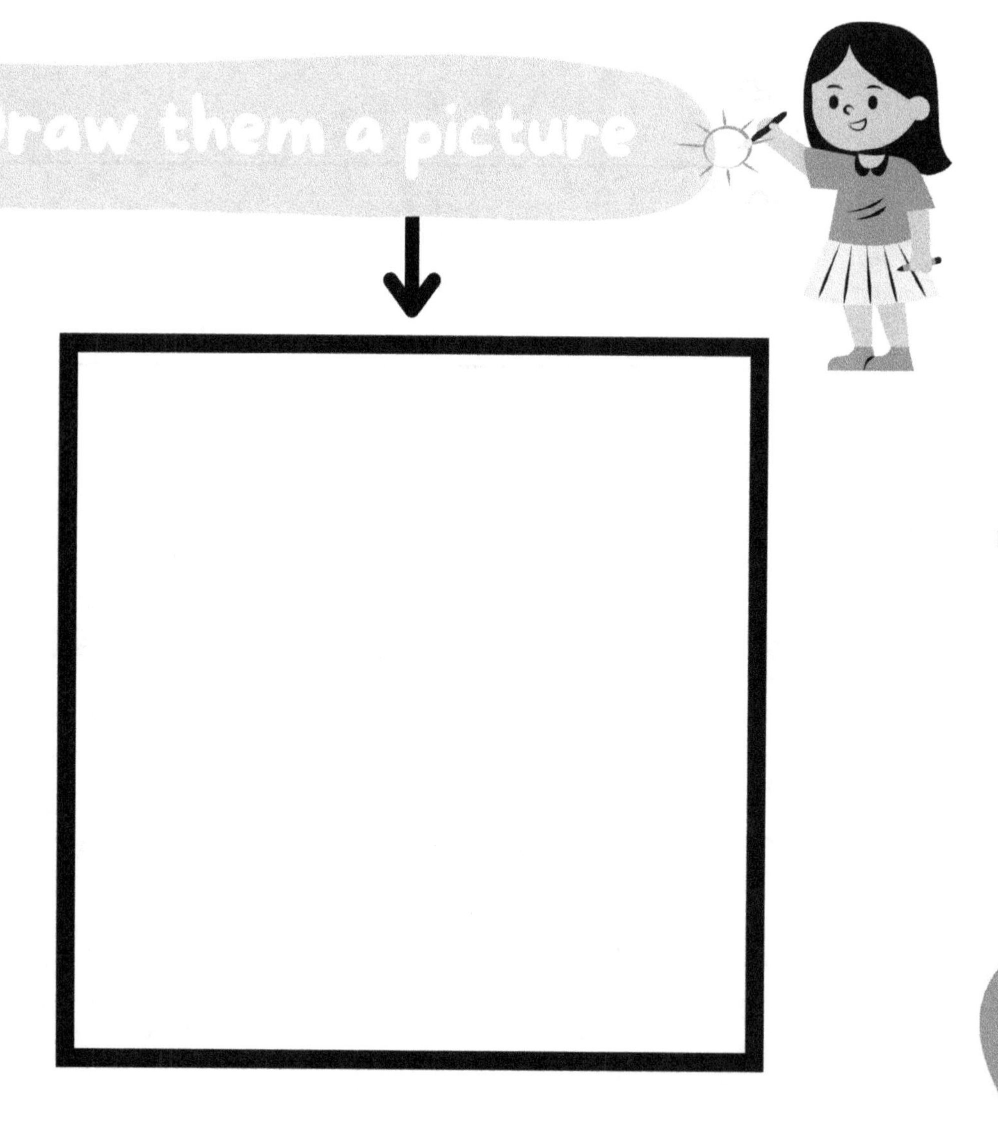

How are you feeling today?

Find the picture or pictures that best describe how you were feeling throughout your day.

PROUD

BORED

CURIOUS

PLAYFUL

TIRED

HUNGRY

ANGRY

WORRIED

SCARED

HAPPY

CONFUSED

NERVOUS

DISGUSTED

ANNOYED

SAD

AMUSED

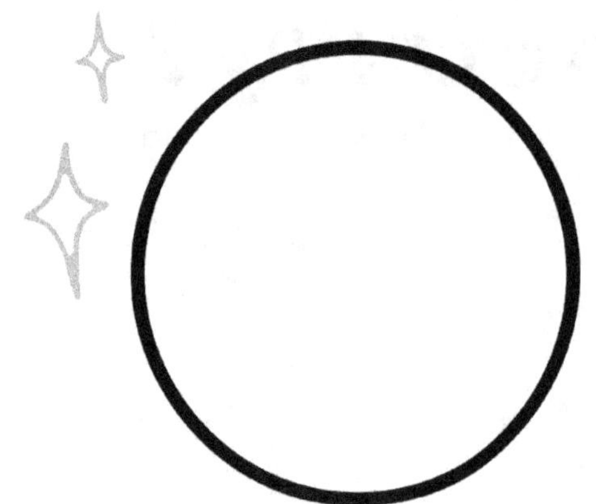

Draw how you made others feel today

BECAUSE I FEEL

I TREATED OTHERS

- - - - - - - - - - -

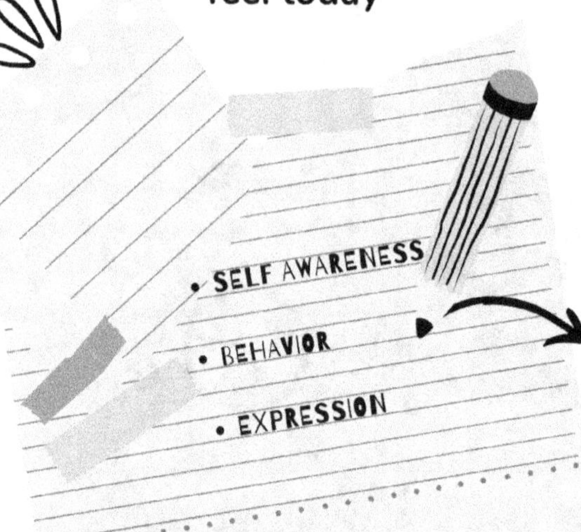

THE BEGINNING

What happened in the beginning to make you feel_______________?

THE MIDDLE

What did you do or say in response?
____
____

How are you treating others now that you feel _______________?

THE END

What was the solution to help you feel better?
____
____

HOW ARE YOU TREATING OTHERS?

I FEEL ____________________________________

BECAUSE ____________________________________

____

____

TO HELP ME FEEL BETTER I AM GOING TO:

____

____

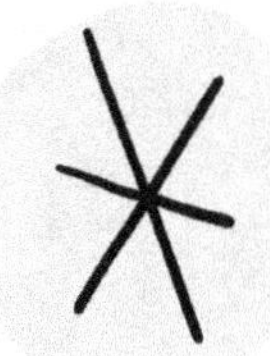

JOURNAL:

DAY 5
FRIENDSHIP FRIDAY

How to be a friend

Play together

Keep promises

Listen to
each other

Work together

Share what
you have

Tell the truth

How are you feeling today?

Find the picture or pictures that best describe how you were feeling throughout your day.

PROUD

BORED

CURIOUS

PLAYFUL

TIRED

HUNGRY

ANGRY

WORRIED

SCARED

HAPPY

CONFUSED

NERVOUS

DISGUSTED

ANNOYED

SAD

AMUSED

(Draw how your friend(s) made you feel today)

TODAY I TOLD MY FRIENDS THEY MADE ME FEEL

- SELF AWARENESS
- BEHAVIOR
- EXPRESSION

HOW ARE YOU PLAYING WITH OTHERS?

THE BEGINNING

What did your friend(s) do in the beginning to make you feel ______________?

THE MIDDLE

What did you do or say in response? ______________

____

How are you treating others now that you feel ______________?

THE END

What was the solution to help you feel better?

____

____

JOURNAL:

My day was: _______________________________

My favorite part was: _______________________

My worst part was: _________________________

My thoughts and concerns
about today:

____

____

____

____

____

Things I can do
to feel better:

____

____

____

____

JOURNAL:

GREAT JOB!!

DON'T FORGET:

- Self Awareness - how do you feel?
- Expression - can you explain why you feel that way?
- Behavior - how are you expressing your feelings to others? (example, if you are sad - are you making others sad?